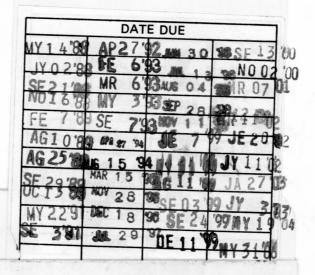

DATE DUE		
MY 1 4 '88	AP 27 '92	JUN 30 '98 SE 13 '00
JY 02 '88	FE 6 '93	JUL 1 3 '98 NO 02 '00
SE 21 '88	MR 6 '93	AUG 04 '98 MR 07 '01
NO 16 '88	MY 3 '93	SEP 28 '98 '02
FE 7 '89	SE 7 '93	NOV 1 1 '02
AG 10 '89	APR 27 '94	JE 7 '99 JE 20 '02
AG 25 '89	AUG 15 94	JY 11 '02
SE 29 '89	MAR 15 '95	AG 11 '99 JA 27 '03
OC 13 '89	NOV 28 '95	SE 03 '99 JY 3 '03
MY 22 '90	DEC 1 8 '96	SE 24 '99 MY 19 '04
SE 3 '91	JUL 29 '97	DE 11 '99 MY 31 '06

HORSES
AND FOALS

HORSES
AND FOALS

by Ellen Rabinowich

Photographs by Joseph F. Viesti

An Easy-Read Fact Book

FRANKLIN WATTS / NEW YORK / LONDON / 1979

Photographs courtesy of Joseph Viesti, with the following exceptions:

American Museum of Natural History, p. 9
International Arabian Horse Association, p. 12
New York Public Library Picture Collection, p. 17
Appaloosa Horse Club, Inc., p. 23
The Palomino Horse Association, Inc., p. 41
Ted Robbins, p. 43

With special thanks to Tim Capps and The Jockey Club in New York

Library of Congress Cataloging in Publication Data

Rabinowich, Ellen
  Horses and foals.

  (An Easy-read fact book)
  Includes index.
  SUMMARY: A brief introduction to the history,
habits, various breeds, care, and training of horses.
  1. Horses—Juvenile literature. [1. Horses.]
I. Viesti, Joseph F.   II. Title.
SF285.R33   636.1   78-16115
ISBN 0-531-02272-2

R.L. 2.9 Spache Revised Formula

6   5   4   3   2   1

This pony is only a few weeks old. Baby ponies and horses, called **foals**, can walk and run soon after they are born. Male foals are called **colts**. Females are called **fillies**.

Foals drink their mother's milk until they are five months old. Animals that feed on their mother's milk, are warm-blooded, and are covered with fur are called **mammals**. The horse is a mammal.

When a foal is about five months old it does not need its mother's milk anymore. Now it eats grass just like its mother does. Horses also eat oats, barley, hay, rye, carrots, and apples.

Full-grown male horses are called **stallions**. Females are called **mares**. Their size is measured from their **withers** (the highest point of their shoulders) to the ground in hands. A **hand** is 4 inches (10.2 cm) or the width of a grown-up's palm. Small horses, called **ponies**, grow no higher than 58 inches (147.3 cm). Some large horses are well over 6 feet (1.8 m) tall and weigh over 2,000 pounds (907 kg)! Horses were not always so big and heavy. Long before there were people, about 60 million years ago, horses were the size of today's dogs. Scientists have named them Eohippus, which means dawn horse. They had toes instead of hooves.

Eohippus

A full-grown horse makes friends with a pony.

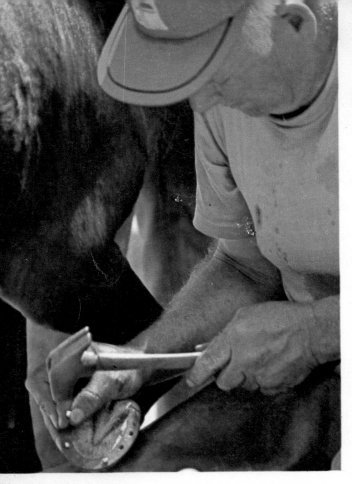

A man gives this horse new shoes.

To get away from their enemies, these little horses had to run quickly. So over millions of years their legs became longer, their bodies heavier, and their toes grew into one hoof. Scientists call our present-day horse by its Latin name—Equus. Their hooves are so strong that nailing on horseshoes, called **shoeing**, does not hurt.

Horses first lived in North America. But after the last Ice Age they suddenly went away. Scientists know that they went to Asia. But how? Did they swim? Horses can swim, but not across oceans. Probably they traveled across a land bridge from Alaska to Asia. Now it is covered with water and is called the Bering Strait.

The Arabian horse has a dish-shaped face.

In Asia and Europe horses kept on changing. Horses living in cold places grew thick, shaggy coats. And those living in the desert became fast and sleek and were able to run for a long time without water. These are the Arabians. They are the oldest living breed.

Those horses living in places without much food grew no bigger than ponies. The Shetland ponies, from Scotland, are very small and strong. But the Falabella pony is the smallest breed of all. When fully grown it stands only 30 inches (76.2 cm) high!

Shetland ponies are often seen at horse shows.

This is a wild Chincoteague pony.

All these horses and ponies were once wild. They lived in large groups. Each group was led by a stallion. Today only Prjevalsky's horses in Asia are truly wild. A few other breeds do run wild, but their ancestors were once tame. They live in England, Ireland, and America.

Sometimes, two stallions fight by getting up on their hindlegs, then kicking and biting.

Scientists believe that cavepeople ate horses. But thousands of years before Christ, the Mesopotamians discovered a better use for them. They trained horses to pull chariots. Today teams of four horses draw buggies in horse shows.

The Greeks often used horses for chariot races during their famous Olympic games. Many Greeks worshiped horses. They had stories about creatures called **centaurs** who were half-man and half-horse and a beautiful winged horse called Pegasus.

Pegasus could fly.

Before cars were invented, people went places by horse.

Soon Europeans discovered that by mating horses of different sizes and strengths, they could produce animals for special purposes. This is called selective breeding. Some horses were bred for their pulling power. These are the **draft breeds**.

In England, Scotland, Belgium, and France draft horses were bred to farm and to pull heavy loads. The largest, called the Shire, is also known as England's National Draft Horse. It took the place of oxen in the fields. The Clydesdales, from Scotland, are known for their high stepping gait. Most draft horses have long tufts of hair on their lower legs. These are called **fetlocks** or **feathers**.

Clydesdales are often seen at horse shows and on television commercials.

Other horses were bred for use in wars. People riding horses had a better chance of winning battles than those on foot. Here the famous Austrian Lipizzaner shows off one of its exciting battle leaps. In the **capriole movement**, it springs from the ground and kicks to stop an attack.

Lipizzaners are also called "high school" horses because they are trained for many years to do hard steps that look like a dance.

Lipizzaners are born with black or dark gray or brown coats, but they change to white or light gray as the horses grow older. However there are several grown-up Lipizzaners in Europe today that are all black.

A white Lipizzaner leaps high.

In Italy, horses are often used at festivals.

Scientists are not sure why horses left North America after the last Ice Age. But they do know that horses were brought back here during the 1500s by Spanish soldiers. They rode horses to explore. When Indians first saw these soldiers on horses they thought they were six-legged gods.

Soon Indians had horses of their own. The Nez Percé tribe bred the Appaloosa. This horse often looks like it's polka dotted or spotted with ink.

The Pintos, brought by the Spaniards, were also ridden by Indians. Because their bodies are brightly splashed with color they are often called paints.

At rodeos cowboys have steer-roping contests.

In the Wild West cowboys made their living on horseback. Horses were used for travel and for herding cattle. Some horses can take one steer from the herd without getting any orders from the rider. These are called **cutting** horses.

Sometimes cowboys fell asleep in the saddle. The horse got home by using its very good memory.

Today there are over one hundred breeds of horses. In most places machines have taken their place for heavy work and war. But horses are still used in many ways.

Horse racing, once called "the sport of kings" in England, is still very popular today. Mostly thoroughbreds are used, and many run faster than 30 mph (48.3 kmph).

Some thoroughbreds do best in **steeplechase races**. In this exciting contest riders used to jump their horses over bushes and fallen trees as they raced through the countryside. The finish line was a church steeple. Today the races are held on specially made courses. This sport is most popular in England.

A horse's three natural ways of moving are the **walk**, **trot**, and **canter** (slow gallop). These are called **gaits**. Today Standardbreeds are bred for harness racing because they are very good at trotting. These horses are also taught another gait called **pacing**.

These Hackneys are wearing blinkers.

Another harness horse, the Hackney, once pulled fancy English carriages. Often it wore leather cups called **blinkers** near its eyes so it would not be bothered by traffic. This is because horses can see in front, to the side, and behind at the same time. Today Hackneys are bred for horse shows.

Quarter horses run the quarter mile faster than any other breed. Because they also can quickly start, turn, and stop, they are often used for polo. In this game they must quickly obey their rider's orders. Polo, once called "hockey on horseback" in England, is still played today.

Horseback riders sometimes show off the quarter horse's great speed and ability to make sharp turns in barrel-racing contests. The horse must gallop around three barrels without knocking them down.

In Mexico some farmers still use horses for plowing.

In many countries all over the world, some horses are still used for work. They help farmers to plow fields, police to hold back crowds, and ranchers to herd cattle.

Other horses are used in ceremonies. The Royal Canadian Mounties police Canada on horseback. They also ride at these special times.

Still other horses are entertainers. Highly trained horses often steal the show at circuses. And untamed ones buck off their riders at rodeos.

However, most horses today are used for pleasure riding. Children often ride Shetland or Welsh ponies because they are gentle.

The strong Welsh pony once worked in coal mines.

Many riders like the American Saddlebreed for its comfortable gait. Because this horse steps high off the ground and carries its tail high, it has been called "the peacock of the horse world."

Some people train their horses for horse shows and jumping. Most horses can jump 3 feet (0.9 m), but some jump as high as 8 feet (2.7 m).

See the white mark on this jumper's face? It is called a **star**. Some horses have a white spot on their noses called a **snip**. If a large stripe runs down the center of their face, it is called a **blaze**.

This horse is a dapple gray.

Many breeds are of different colors. There are pure white Albinos, reddish-brown bays, tan-colored duns, chestnuts, browns, blacks, and dapple grays.

This horse is a golden Palomino. Roy Rogers' horse, Trigger, was a Palomino too.

Another famous horse was a black English carriage horse. It is the star of Anna Sewell's book—*Black Beauty*.

All horses must be groomed each day to make their coats shine. Usually people use a comb, curry brush, and rub rag. But if the horse is very muddy sometimes it is watered down.

People who know a lot about horses can tell how old a horse is by looking at its teeth. As the horse grows older, the enamel ridges of its teeth wear down. Many horses live about twenty years, but one horse lived to be sixty-two!

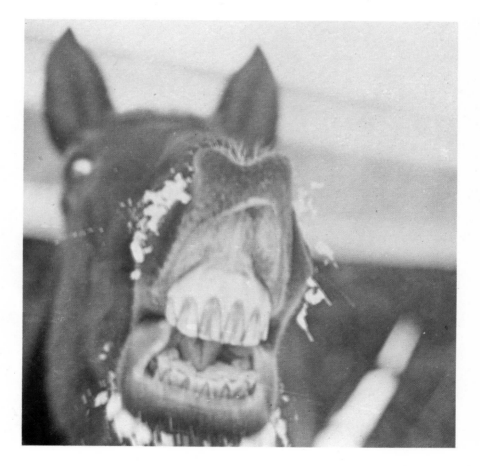

Riding may be learned on an English or Western saddle. Western saddles are big and heavy and have a saddle horn. English saddles are lighter and are often used by pleasure riders. Some people like to ride sidesaddle and some like bareback, with no saddle at all.

A very young sidesaddle rider gets ready for a show.

Riding is lots of fun and also good exercise for both horse and rider. Most horses need at least two hours of exercise each day. After riding, a person should walk a horse until it cools off.

Children often make very good riders.

Many people of all ages love horses. Here a young boy makes friends with a very young foal.

INDEX

ABOUT THE AUTHOR

The author of several books for young readers, Ellen Rabinowich has also acted professionally and produced a dramatic film feature. She is the author of *Kangaroos, Koalas, and Other Marsupials* in the Franklin Watts First Book series, and is currently working on a book about sea lions, seals, and walruses. Ms. Rabinowich lives and works in New York City.